THE REAL RULES FOR GIRLS

BY **MINDY MORGENSTERN**
DESIGNED BY AMY INOUYE
CREATIVE CONCEPT BY MARI FLORENCE

POCKET BOOKS
New York London Toronto Sydney Singapore

POCKET BOOKS
1230 Avenue of the Americas
New York, NY 10020

Published by arrangement with 17th Street Productions, Inc., An Alloy Company

ISBN: 0-7434-5725-0

First Pocket Books trade paperback printing June 2002

10 9 8 7 6 5 4 3 2 1

Cover design by Amy Inouye

Printed in the U.S.A.

THE REAL RULES FOR GIRLS

CONT

ROMANCE

WORK

SOCIAL LIFE

ENTS

FAMILY

MONEY

LIFE TIPS

Acknowledgments

The author wishes to thank the following for their inspiration and support and because they'd never talk to her again if she didn't:

Valerie Ahern, Kacee Colter, Courteney Cox Arquette, Pamela Eells, Katie Ford, Kelly Breidenbach Elliott, Amy Inouye, Joanna Johnson, Debbee Klein, Pierre Brogan and Paradigm Talent & Literary Agency, Carl Halverson Haley, Terry Maloney Haley & Corbin Jon Haley, Kelly Hommon, Nicholas Hope & Jamie Wooten, Phyllis Landres, Catherine MacNeil, Christian McLaughlin, Janet, Andrew & Benjamin Morgenstern, Barbara Morgenstern, Lanny & Bryant Moyer, Nancylee Myatt, Pam Nelson, Dr. Lucy Postolov, Tom Power, Claire Rifkin Aronowitz, Hope Royaltey, Ashley Sabille, Mary Kaye Schilling, Israel Segal & Dane Holweger, Marla Svoboda-Stel, Bill Veloric.

If you obey all the rules

you miss all the fun.

—KATHARINE HEPBURN

I'm proud to say I was the first person to utter the dreaded "P" word on television. That's right—"period," and I don't mean the punctuation mark. That was my small (but significant!) contribution to feminism.

All right, so I'm not Gloria Steinem. But let's face it—the only preparation we got for the arrival of our first period were the directions on the back of a box of "feminine products." Was there anything more confusing? We were more embarrassed about the onset of "womanhood" than ever.

Wouldn't it have been great if someone would have told us the truth? That your period can be a big fat drag, but that it's ultimately kind of cool since it means being able to have babies? But that hip attitude was impossible at the time, because we lived in a world in which the P-Word was weird and shameful. So that's why I *am* glad that I was the first one to toss it off casually on network TV.

And while we're at it, I wish someone would have told me the truth about a *lot* of things when I was growing up. Life would have been so much easier if someone had sat me down and told me *The Real Rules:*

That the guy you thought was "all that" when you were thirteen would make you gag when you're thirty. That the road to your dream job is filled with lots of sucky jobs along the way . . . That's the stuff no one tells you when you're a kid.

And that's what this book aims to do—to tip off girls to the truth about topics which were so *dimly lit* for my generation, and still are for girls today. We need to tell girls that it's possible to follow your dream and figure out a way to pay the bills, and that your mother will always make you crazy, but you'll learn to deal with it.

Of course, our parents *tried* to tell us those things, but in a different way, and in a different time. Now it's the turn of my generation to lend a hand to the next crop of girls, with advice based on our own experience—and on a very different world. You and I can make things a bit easier for our daughters, nieces, goddaughters, and granddaughters. Let's break the silence and tell them *The Real Rules.* And hey, we may even be reminded of a few things we've forgotten ourselves.

—Courteney Cox Arquette

ROMANCE

There's a lid for
every pot.

OKAY, I KNOW IT SOUNDS TOTALLY LAME, BUT IT'S SOMETHING MY GRANDMA USED TO TELL ME WHEN I'D WORRY ABOUT FINDING MY LIFE PARTNER. What she meant was: *there's someone for everyone.* I gotta tell you, her old-world sentiment was a comfort when I was feeling hopeless about dating. That and her Velveeta cheese casseroles, but that's another story.

A couple of years ago, I was over at my friend Kelly's and we were cooking pasta carbonatta—which is not an easy task, by the way—when we realized that we needed a lid for the pasta pot. Well, we looked everywhere but it turned out she didn't have the lid-mate, and, to tell the truth, I panicked.

Had Grandma lied to me? Had I been building my romantic hopes on a total lie? Then I thought: No, that lid is probably sitting alone and unused in someone else's cabinet without its pot-partner. Oh sure, it might be used as a *substitute* every once in a while when another lid was dirty, but it never *really* fit in with the other pots and it knew it.

And then it occurred to me—what we as a nation must do is free all of the single lids and pots so that they may find each other and be happy. I said to Kelly: That's what we as single babes have to do, too! Free ourselves from our "cabinets" and get out there and find the lid for our pot! She looked at me kinda weird, but then totally agreed. So, we put on some lipstick and went out to find our soulmates.

In fact, we were so excited about our mission that we forgot to turn the pasta off, and now I can't even *apply* for fire insurance until the year 2050. But I didn't care because we had met so many cool people that night. So remember: If you're a pot you *will* find your lid one day, or vice versa . . . *you* know what I mean.

Just remember to turn the stove off.

You should
always be
driving,
even from
the backseat.

Dating guys should not be a painful experience—mentally, emotionally or physically. If a guy is verbally abusive or hits you, he's a BAD GLY. Even if he says he loves you. Get out! Ask a teacher, counselor, or parent for help right away.

JUST REMEMBER THIS: IF YOU'RE GETTING PRESSURED TO DO IT—WE'RE TALKING ANYWHERE FROM HAND-HOLDING TO HOME BASE—DON'T DO IT. That's because someone pressuring you to do something before you're ready is *always* wrong. Even if they tell you they love you, even if your best friend has already done it, even if they tell everyone you're a loser for not doing it. This has got to be your idea.

It is possible that blondes prefer gentlemen.

—*Mamie Van Doren*

There is
no
Happily Ever
After.

I KNOW THAT'S A BIT HARSH, BUT I'M ONLY TRYING TO PREPARE YOU FOR THE REALISTIC SIDE OF LONG-TERM ROMANCE—IT'S NOT LIKE WHAT YOU'VE SEEN IN THE MOVIES. Take *An Officer and a Gentleman* for example. Okay, you know the end where Richard Gere struts into the paper bag factory where Debra Winger works, picks her up and carries her off into the sunset? You're left to believe they lived happily ever after, right? Cha! If there were ever a sequel, this is how it would be:

> *Debbie weighs about three hundred pounds; overweight after having four whiney kids. She yells at Rich all day about his drinking. They fight constantly about the fact that he can't hold down a job, and they're forced to eat Hamburger Helper . . . without the hamburger.*

Okay, maybe I went too far. (*Me, go too far?*) But the fact remains that no relationship is perfect.

But here's the good news: You CAN have a dreamy relationship. Just remember that it's a package deal: along with the romantic days filled with champagne and sunsets come the UNromantic days when you're both tired of one another and one of you has bad breath. A couple in a strong relationship can work through the good, the bad and the ugly.

Love yourself first and everything else falls into line. You really have to love yourself to get anything done in this world. —Lucille Ball

Don't rain on my parade. —Barbra Streisand

Lead your own

conga band.

YOU KNOW WAY BACK IN THE OLDEN DAYS LIKE ON ***I LOVE LUCY*** WHEN ETHEL WOULD INTRODUCE LUCY AS "MRS. RICKY RICARDO," INSTEAD OF "LUCY RICARDO?" Well, that's 'cause Lucy was considered the "little missus." Everyone was supposed to pretend that she didn't have a real identity apart from being Ricky's wife. This was *totally* strange since, after all, the show's called *I Love Lucy*. (Like, Hello? Who's the star here?) But back in the '50s, people bought into the idea that Lucy was successful only if her husband Ricky was. Weird.

Although you don't hear women calling themselves "Mrs. John Jones" or whatever today, we still might think in the same terms and not even know it. C'mon, we've all lived through some version of: *That guy is so cool. If only he'd ask me out, I know I'd be, too.* What I'm saying is—*you* could be the Ricky (Rickina?) Ricardo, leading the conga band down at the Tropicana. Then you'll be cool, 'cause you've done it for yourself.

Following a precedent is an easy substitute for thinking.

—RUTH SMELTZER

The football captains of today are the burger jockeys of tomorrow.

OKAY, TODAY YOU'RE SAYING YOU JUST GOTTA SPEND THE REST OF YOUR LIFE WITH THE COOLEST, MOST STUDLY GUY AT SCHOOL OR YOU'LL DIE. But trust me, in ten or fifteen years, you'll be riding in the back of a limo, having just received the Nobel Peace Prize, and on your way to the Democratic Convention to accept your party's nomination for President, when suddenly and without warning, you will become very hungry. You won't have much time between events so you'll tell Jeeves to pull the limo over while you pop into Mickey Dee's for a little nosh. On the way in, you'll think about ordering the chicken sandwich without the bun, rationalizing that you'll save the calories so you can get the chocolate milkshake, guilt-free.

That decision made, you'll confidently dash through the Golden Arches looking totally hot in your $3,000 Versace suit that Donatella insisted she design especially for you. You'll reach the counter while hastily rummaging through your Dolce and Gabbana looking for something smaller than a 'hundred,' when something will tell you to look up.

Your eyes will lock instantly, he'll smile at you, and you'll smile back 'cause you're never rude, and you'll think to yourself, *Hey that balding Assistant Manager who just asked me if I want to "Super-Size that" looks awfully familiar.* Then it will hit you like a ton of bricks: It's what's-his-name from tenth grade—the guy you thought you couldn't live without. At which point, you will drop to your knees, not caring that some kid has totally spewed his Happy Meal on the floor right in front of you, and thank God you listened to your Aunt Mindy and refused to give up your own dreams for his.

What the world really needs is more love and less paperwork. —Pearl Bailey

You be
the judge,
Judy.

THIS APPLIES TO ANY SITUATION, NOT JUST TO GUYS. But if you're like me you've spent WAY too much time worrying about what other people think of you. The deal is, everyone has their own point of view (my therapist calls it "perspective"), and you know what? We can't really change what goes on in the heads of other people. Sure, you can argue and tap dance until someone lets you have your way, but you can't really affect the basic way that other people think. And believe me, *I've tried . . . and tried.*

After twelve years of therapy and fifty thousand dollars, I've learned that we can only control what *we* think. (And by "we" I don't mean me and my many personalities. I mean you and me, you sassy wenches.) So, fellow *control enthusiasts**, next time you're re-living an embarrassing moment imagining that your wildest crush thinks you're a total freak, gain control by asking yourself what *you* think about *him*.

**such a nicer term than "control freak"—don't you agree?*

YOUR FIRST BOYFRIEND SHOULD BE LIKE THE FIRST PANCAKE. JUST A TESTER TO SEE IF THE GRIDDLE IS HOT ENOUGH.

Think big. Travel outside your comfort zones.

WORK

So jump
already.

Put a cap on your decision process—set a deadline. Most power divas cite this as a top success secret: Knowing how to make a fast decision. (And not looking back to second-guess. Who has time?)

HERE'S THE DEAL: IN LIFE, YOU WILL BE FACED WITH THOUSANDS OF DECISIONS. Most will be along the lines of: *Which flavor dental floss should I use?* And some will be more important, like: *The lightning's three whole miles away. Do I really need to put the top up on the convertible?*

But the truth is, there are few "right or wrong" decisions that are absolutely clear. Hardly any mistakes are really fatal—okay, maybe if you're a doctor or a pilot. But for the rest of us, most decisions are subjective. *Should I keep my boring, dependable day job or throw caution to the wind and try my hand as a chef? Should I go to graduate school or get a full-time job?* Important decisions—yes! But don't agonize over them so much that you miss out on life or make yourself crazy.

Keep moving! Remember: For most choices, the only wrong move you can make is to *not make one at all.*

n to network. Find out how others can help you or vice versa.

Do what you love.

UNLESS YOU'RE AN HEIRESS OR YOU WIN THE LOTTERY, YOU'RE GOING TO BE SPENDING 50% OF YOUR LIFE WORKING. Doesn't that suck? I mean, isn't that great? And since 50% is, well, half your life, shouldn't you do something you love? It would be a bummer to spend eight to twelve hours a day, fifty weeks a year for forty years working just to pay the rent, wouldn't it?

You may not know this very second what you'd like to do for the rest of your life, but you can take the first steps to find out. Here are some tips: Write down what you like/love to do in your spare time.

Play soccer after school? I bet that's how Mia Hamm and Brandy Chastain started their careers as a professional soccer players. Or, if you love sports but hate to sweat, think about becoming a sportscaster.

Love to draw? There are graphic artists, storyboard artists, fine artists, and cartoonists who started out just like you, doodling mindlessly on your brother's term paper.

Have a green thumb? Maybe you should have a doctor look at it. If it's not thumb-rot, think about becoming a florist, botanist, or landscape artist.

Once you have some ideas, you can surf the net or go to the library and find out how to make a living by using your talent. It's hard to imagine the future and how you're going to fit into it. But don't sweat it. You have lots of time to figure it out, and you can even change your mind a thousand times before you know for sure.

Everyone's as scared as you are. Trust me, the suits are bluffing, too.

Ask questions. Expand your horizons by raising your hand.

A good bluff
can get you
anywhere.

SINCE ATTITUDE IS EVERYTHING, LET'S TALK ABOUT THE BENEFITS OF BLUFFING. In a poker game, you can win a hand even if you have lousy cards. It's all about making the other players THINK you have a winning hand. It sounds like a lie, but it's not—it's a bluff! So if you're a good bluffer you can *psych out* your friends until they fold, and then rake in the pot.

Now, out in the real world, I'm not saying that you should *lie* about your actual skills—just that it never hurts to bite off a bit more than you can chew. For example, if your boss asks you to put together a marketing campaign—say yes!

So what if you've never done it before—*you* know that you can learn, and learn fast. Sure you might panic later—but we all need a little panic as motivation from time to time.

Let's recap, shall we?

♠ DO bluff if someone asks you to do something you can learn quickly.

♣ DON'T bluff about your ability to perform very specific tasks, like heart surgery.

♥ DO bluff about your level of confidence (if need be).

♦ DON'T bluff about explicit experience. (Example: Don't make up stuff on your resumé—that's lying!)

I have yet to hear a man ask for advice on how to combine marriage and a career.

—GLORIA STEINEM

Jobs will suck along the way.

YOU'LL HAVE LOTS OF SUCKY JOBS ON THE WAY TO YOUR DREAM JOB. I totally did. I hated being a secretary or production assistant, but looking back, I learned valuable things that later helped me when I became a television writer.

Here's a great example taken from the archives of my very own life. Once a director I worked for (he will remain nameless, but for our purposes, let's call him Baldy) phoned me at SIX in the morning. SIX! Baldy told me his son (let's call him The Midget) was sick and asked if I would come to his house and take The Midget's stool sample to the lab for testing. And I said NO WAY!!! That's DIS-gusting! (This IS a true story. I swear.)

Well, Baldy was really mad at me and tortured me at work for the next two weeks. I should just quit, I thought. How is being tormented by this talent-free loser going to help me be a writer? But looking back on the experience, it *did* help me. I paid the bills and I made some great contacts in that sucky job.

And how's this for karma? Some years later, my friend who worked for a magazine called to tell me she was writing an article about celebrities and asked me if I had any "tell all" stories about famous Hollywood people. I told her the Baldy/Midget story and she published it. I was kinda famous for a while, and I felt totally vindicated since I got back at Baldy. Baldy later sued me for everything I was worth. (I AM kidding about that.)

The point is, we all have to pay our dues in one way or another. Just know you won't have some crappy job forever; just take what you need from it. Remember—it's just a stepping stone to the place you want to be.

Compliments
won't pay for
the Porsche.

MOST OF YOU WILL BE OUT IN THE WORKING WORLD SOMEDAY SOON. So I'd like for you to think of your talent as a commodity, like a television set. Let's say a brand new 45" Sony Wide Screen High Definition TV—the really hot kind that are flat and hang on the wall like a picture. With a built-in VCR and Surroundsound. Okay, I've gone over the edge, but stay with me.

Now, if your business was selling TV sets, would you just give away all your 45" Sony Wide Screen High Definition TVs? No way! You'd be out of business in no time. See what I'm driving at?

No? Let me be more direct. During the course of your career, you will be in *lots* of meetings where *every*one's smiling at you and *every*one's agreed that you are beyond brilliant. And you'll be smiling too, basking in the fuzzy warm feeling of it all, when suddenly you'll realize: *HEY! No one's offering to pay me here!* And that's when it will be your job to *ask to be paid*. You'll learn to do it in a charming way, believe me, but you'll learn to make it clear that your TV sets with all the bells and whistles aren't free.

It may be difficult to demand what you're worth, because you don't want to rock the boat, and you want to be liked. But the big girls and boys out there in the business world will respect you more if you respect yourself.

It's nice to be liked,

BUT IT'S BETTER TO BE PAID.

—Liz Phair

**If there
isn't a door,
kick in a wall.**

IF THE DOOR IS LOCKED, TURN THE KEY. If the key won't turn, get a battering ram. If you can't knock down the door, look for a window. What I'm cleverly trying to say here is that opportunity knocks, but not always on doors. Still confused? Now you know how I feel on a daily basis.

Okay, forget the door/window thing. The point I'm trying to make is that you've got to create your own opportunities.

Consider, for example, my friend who dreamed of being a screenwriter. She wrote script after script, peddled them to every studio in Hollywood, but no one wanted to buy them. Did she curse show business? Did she think of quitting? Did she kick her feet, pound her fists and pull out her hair? Well . . . yes she did. But after she calmed down, and her hair grew back, she thought: *Heck, I'll turn one of my scripts into a movie myself!*

She used some of her own savings, borrowed from her parents, charged up her credit cards, found a director, crew, and actors and started shooting. It took a couple of years to complete because everyone was working for free and they ran out of $$$ a couple of times, but eventually, it was a done deal. She entered her movie into film festivals all over the world, and it even won some awards.

The thing is, my friend didn't wait for something to happen, she *made* it happen. And that's what you'll have to do, too. Wanna be your own boss? Start a business now. Wanna be an actor? Start your own playhouse. That kind of creative thinking (and hard work) will get you everywhere.

If you don't like something, change it.
If you can't change it, change your attitude.
Don't complain.

—Maya Angelou

Your way isn't the only right way.

IF YOU'RE LIKE ME, YOU'RE RIGHT ABOUT EVERYTHING. I know, I know—it's a terrible burden. For years I've felt the pressure of explaining to people—at length if necessary—the way that *everything* should be done. I told taxi drivers how to drive *(I knew the fastest route!)*; I told waiters how to wait *(dressing on the side!)*; I told my friends who to date *(lose the loser!)*. I wasn't being bossy—I was being helpful! If only everyone could only be as right as me . . .

So, you can imagine my surprise when, as a grown-up in the business world, I discovered that other people's ideas could be just as right as mine. Of course I was in a headlock at the time, butcha know . . . What I had to learn the hard way was that a good girl boss listens to everyone's ideas before making the final decision. Sometimes you'll choose to go with someone else's idea because it *is* better than yours, or maybe because it's a good political move (the boss's daughter came up with it), or it's good for morale. *(Boy, she's cool 'cause she listens to the little people.)* And look at it this way: You can take total credit for being the one who hired all these geniuses.

Life is to be lived.
If you have to support yourself,
you had bloody well better
find some way that is going
to be interesting.

—KATHARINE HEPBURN

Other women are not the enemy.

OKAY, WELL MAYBE *THIS* WOMAN. She's pretty creepy. And, unfortunately, you'll find some women like this in the business world who act like there's room for only one girl boss. It's like there's only one big Lady Ladder and they're at the top, fending the rest of us off with their tasteless Manolo Blahnik knockoffs.

Boy, they must be exhausted. I'm tired just typing about it. It's totally playing into this old, outdated idea that is so uncool. Like there's not enough to go around. You, future girl bosses of the world, must stop the cycle.

The truth is that most of us *like* working together, and what's more, we like to see each other become successful. It's high time there was a "grrl's club" where we stuck together no matter what. If we're fighting each other constantly, we'll all lose, but if we're all in it together, who knows what amazing things we'll accomplish?

It never hurts
to kiss up.

When speaking to others, especially adults, look 'em straight in the eye . . . without looking like a stalker.

EVERYONE LOVES TO BE FLATTERED, EVEN WHEN THEY KNOW YOU'RE KISSING UP. Do it sparingly and with discretion. Even if you think you'll hurl in the process.

PICK YOUR BATTLES.

HERE'S A LITTLE SECRET: The key to being a Power Negotiating Babe isn't knowing what to fight for, it's knowing *what to give away*. Before you walk into any room to hash out a deal, figure out two or three points that you're willing to concede. Hey, throw in points you've made up and pretend they mean the world to you: i.e., *Aunt Gert gets a multi-million dollar, two-picture deal with an office on the studio lot or I'm walking*. That'll give you the leverage to keep the stuff that really matters. (And if they do give "Aunt Gert" that contract, go check her out of the retirement home in Boca Raton, prop her up in the director's chair, teach her how to say "Action!" and you've got it made.)

Most models' careers are over at 23.

Go with

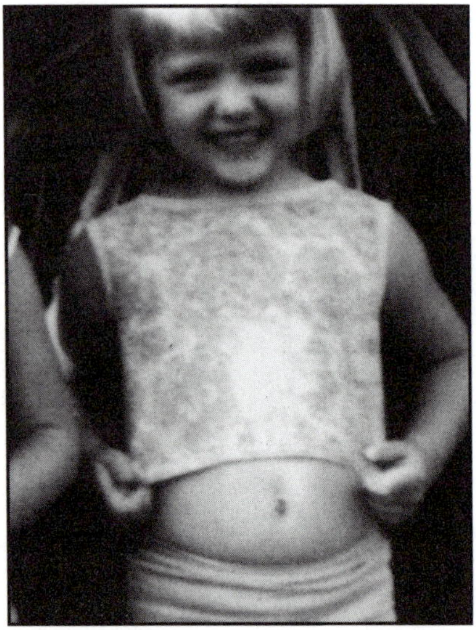

your gut.

 Take responsibility for your feelings and actions. Others can't *make* you do or feel what you don't want to do or feel. Eleanor Roosevelt once said, *"No one can make you feel inferior without your consent."*

TRUST YOURSELF! I guarantee that it will give you more confidence and, eventually, success. Believe me, I've gone the low self-esteem/misery route and it's not as glamorous as it sounds.

Here's an embarrassing example from the Mindy files. Back when I was twelve (let's just say a few years ago, shall we?), my mom made me take ballet. This was a particularly bizarre impulse on her part, since I was, well, on the clumsy side. Anyway, because I totally didn't trust myself to remember the routines, I would follow the girl in front of me, who was a really good dancer. You know the type—perfect ballerina, got all the leads, blah, blah, blah. It goes without saying that I hated her.

Well, one day in class I was "dancing" in the row behind the Perfect One, following her moves and thinking I was doing a pretty good job. Then, without warning, Herself totally bungled the routine and—because I was following her—I bungled it too. But who did the teacher see screw up? Not her perfect pet, *no*, it was klutzy me. So I had to stay after class and work with the teacher alone. I was *totally* embarrassed, plus I missed out on going to see a Pippi Longstocking movie with all my friends.

The point is, don't take ballet. Just kidding—the point is you're never going to be perfect. Eventually, you're bound to goof up some routine. (You're human, after all.) But you'll goof up a lot less if you *trust yourself*. And if you do make a mistake, at least it'll be *yours* and not the Dancing Queen's in the front row.

I can change my life. No one can do it for me. —Carol Burnett

No drama queens
in the office.

Brush, floss, see a dentist every six months. Repeat.

THINK ABOUT HOW YOU COMPETE IN SPORTS. Chances are, it's a war when you're in the middle of a game, but once it's over, you all head off to the locker room to compare trig homework. *(Editor's note: We never encourage comparison of trig homework. Writer's note: Well, I sucked at trig.)*

What I'm saying is that when you're in the throws of the game, focus on your work and on the goal. Put your heart and soul into it when required, but when the game's over, let it go!

90% OF SUCCESS IS JUST SHOWING UP.

WELL, YOU DON'T HAVE ANY CHANCE IF YOU STAY IN BED WITH THE COVERS PULLED UP OVER YOUR HEAD.

Do the hardest thing on Earth for you.

—*Katherine Mansfield*

SOCIAL

LIFE

Cut your friends
a break.

TRUST ME, THERE WILL COME A TIME WHEN YOUR BEST FRIEND—YES, THE ONE YOU DID THE *FRIENDS FOREVER* PACT WITH—WILL DO SOMETHING TO YOU THAT REALLY CHAPS YOUR BUTT. Something you think you can never forgive, like the time my best friend (name withheld to protect the guilty) told my deepest darkest secret about my crush (name withheld to protect a jerk) to my BROTHER (well, there's no protecting him) when she knew that the little bro would go *straight* to the jerk, and spill all.

Well, I guess I'm still a little sensitive about that one. But what's important is that Julie (oops!) and I did stay friends. (Well, after she apologized for THREE straight days, told me TWO humiliating things about herself which I was officially allowed to spread AND ran naked in front of the entire school during half-time at the homecoming game. It was only after the police arrested her for indecent exposure that I began to feel a little better.) After all, I figured that Julie was only trying to get me a date (if in a totally cheesy way). And on further thought, I surmised that one day even *I* was bound to make a dumb mistake with a friend, and I'd be glad if she were smart enough to forgive *me*.

Really good people are few and far between—don't let them go because of dumb mistakes or misunderstandings. The best friendships allow for a little flakiness. (I figure the ratio is about one flaky thing per twenty-five years.)

People are more fun than anybody. —Dorothy Parker

Listen to your friends
even when you think your ears will fall off.
After all, you'll want your friends
to listen to you when you're whining,
uh, er, droning on endlessly,
er, you know what I mean.

You don't have to have all the answers.

Three tricks when speaking to others: **1.** Be nice first, instead of waiting to see if others will be nice to you. Defensiveness is not attractive. **2.** If you don't know what to say, listen. **3.** Remember, everyone loves to talk about themselves, so ask questions.

SOMETIMES FRIENDS JUST WANT TO VENT, AND DON'T NEED YOU TO SOLVE THEIR PROBLEMS. Other times they'll vent *and* really need your help. There will be times when they'll need you to come up with a Plan of Action (*"First, we'll have to let the air out his tires . . ."*). But lots of other times they'll just need you to sit there and look sympathetic. In which case you might throw in a comforting comment or two (*"What a witch!"* or *"Yeah, he's the only guy I know who wears black and* still *looks fat"*). But most of all, this is your chance to offer sisterly support, not brainy advice.

I'm not offended by all the dumb blonde jokes because I know I'm not dumb . . . and I also know that I'm not blonde.

—DOLLY PARTON

When it comes to friends, know your Pumas from your pumps.

Don't fake knowledge. You'll really look stupid if you try to talk about something you know nothing about. But you can always BE OPEN. (*"I don't know anything about opera, but I'd love to go."*)

I THINK I CAN SUM UP THIS WHOLE DEAL WITH THE 'OLE SHOE METAPHOR. Okay, your tennis shoes are like your good friends—comfy and worn in. They go with practically everything you own, so you wear them everyday. And acquaintances are like your heels. Even though they're a snacky pair of pumps, you only wear them a couple of times a year. I mean, if you wore them everyday, you'd have blisters, right?

Here's the deal: You'll know lots of different people in your life—almost everyone can enrich you in some way. Maybe there is someone who won't be a BF, but who knows a lot about art and is a really cool museum-partner from time to time. That's a great acquaintance (*snacky pair of pumps*)—just don't expect the same stuff from him/her as you would from a best friend (*comfy tennies*). Then you'll avoid being disappointed. You can have a fun time chatting about Picasso's Blue Period *without* getting any blisters. Get it?

It's the good girls who keep diaries; the bad girls never have the time.

—Tallulah Bankhead

Just go
to the
damn party.

TAKE IT FROM ME, A WORLD-CLASS COUCH QUEEN—I CAN ALWAYS THINK OF A MILLION REASONS *NOT* TO GO TO A PARTY. So much effort is involved. Hair, make-up, wardrobe, crisis therapy . . . It's such a production. Why, it's like starring in a movie! (But without the $7 million salary. Then it would be worth it.) Sometimes it seems so much easier to stay at home with *Nick at Nite,* especially if you're worried about who'll be at the party, and whether they'll look better than you.

Here's a hint: JUST GO. There are so many GREAT reasons why you should, even if you don't want to. Here are some reasons why: Because you might (a) have fun with your friends; (b) encounter your soul mate over the cheese dip; (c) meet a business contact who wouldn't otherwise let you into her office; or (d) get some free food.

More helpful hints from the *Secret Mindy Party Tips* file to put you at ease:

- Make a "fall-back" plan for later (like seeing a movie) in case the party really sucks.
- Call around ahead of time to find someone you can glom on to when you get there.
- When at the party: Get over yourself, everyone is NOT staring at you (unless you have toilet paper stuck to your shoe).
- Before entering a party, check shoes for toilet paper.

Life is a banquet, and most poor suckers are starving to death!

—AUNTIE MAME

Learn how to
work a room.

LEMME FILL YOU IN ON A LITTLE SECRET: MOST PEOPLE GET THE JITTERS BEFORE THEY WALK INTO A PARTY. It's all about attitude, my friends. So learn how to enter a room. You've got to come in with confidence (dig deep), take a big breath, and make your presence known. Remember, you only have one time to make a first impression.

So, when I go to a party, I like to pretend I'm not me. What I mean is, I'm shy when it comes to social situations, so I like to "act" or "pretend" I'm someone confident walking into the party—like an actor taking on a role. Try to emulate the personality of a friend or a movie star who's got it going on. How can you fail if you're Cameron Diaz?

Don't compromise yourself. You're all you've got.

—JANIS JOPLIN

3 THINGS THAT SEEM SIMPLE BUT AREN'T

EVERY GIRL SHOULD LEARN TO:

ASK FOR HELP

No matter how strong you are, you can't do everything yourself. Friends feel rejected if you don't let them help you. Learn how to accept favors as graciously as you offer them.

ACCEPT A COMPLIMENT

Think of it this way: You insult people if you don't agree with them.

TURN SOMEONE DOWN WITH GRACE

If someone asks you out on a date or wants you to work for them, you'd say they have great taste, right? So even if you're not interested, return the favor by being gracious. Say *"Thanks, I'd love to go out with you (work for you)—I'm flattered. But I've already got a date (job I love)"*— even if you don't feel that way. Never burn a bridge.

EVERY GIRL'S SURE-FIRE TIPS FOR WORKING A PARTY

✓ **WORK UP A CONVERSATION STARTER.**

It's not like you have to write anything down. On your way to the party, think about who's gonna be there and imagine how you could chat them up. If Steve is gonna be there, and you worked with him on the school paper, it might be something like *"Steve! Hold on to your veggie burger, I've got to tell you this freaky thing I heard about the new editor!"* Only not as nerdy, and not so loud, just in case the new editor is there. You get the idea. That's what they call a "sense of purpose" (read: *confidence*) and you'll be amazed how it can help you work a room.

✓ **DESPITE WHAT YOUR MOTHER TOLD YOU, *TALK TO STRANGERS.***

This is a toughie, but there's a trick to this one, too. The same "sense of purpose" thing can apply here as well. If there's an interesting looking girl you'd like to chat up, find something definite to ask her about. *"Hey, that's a cool cargo bag—where'd you get it?"* And take it from there. Trust me—it works! Everyone loves to be admired.

✓ **WHEN EVERYTHING ELSE FAILS, FIND THE HOSTESS, THE DOG OR THE FOOD.**

Even with these sure-fire tricks, there may come moments when you falter. You're there alone, feeling stupid by yourself. Don't run! Regain your confidence by finding a task. Look for the girl who invited you to the party. (This gives you a reason to ask a bunch of people if they've seen her. And finally, when you do find her, you have someone to talk to.) If you can't find her—glom onto the dog, and play catch like you've never played catch before. Or go searching for the food or something to drink. Again, it's a way to have a task, and talk to other people. (*"Hey—where'd you find those pigs in a blanket?"*)

✓ *And if you're shy, don't forget to pretend you're Cameron Diaz.*

It never hurts
to make
a fool
of yourself.

I SUBSCRIBE TO THE THOUGHT THAT IT'S BETTER TO GO TOO FAR THAN NOT FAR ENOUGH. Life is for the living, so live it big and to the fullest. Sure, you'll go overboard sometimes and embarrass yourself—so what?

A cool teacher in my young life (and I've been blessed with so many, but she probably was my favorite, Lanny Moyer. Topeka High School rocks!) once had everyone in my class write an obituary. It sounds kinda morbid, I know, but it gave me pause to think about what I wanted to have accomplished when it was all through. I probably wrote something like:

> *Hollywood hotty, the beautiful, talented, universally revered and lusted-after Mindy Morgenstern passed away in her sleep today in her million-dollar bed on the smaller of her six islands in the Caribbean. She was 120. Though her beginnings were humble, she followed her dream by moving to Hollywood after college, winning the Oscar and Emmy many times over for both her acting and for her writing (well, this obit is proof). After collecting so many statuettes she was heard to remark, "There's not a shelf strong enough to hold all my talent."*

Blah, blah, blah. But you get the picture! Writing your obit is a great reminder that you only live once, as they say, so don't be afraid to take a few chances. SO WHAT if you fall on your face from time to time? That's the only way you'll learn. It's your life—do it right!

Behind every successful man is a surprised woman. —MARYON PEARSON

Don't screw up a
good friendship
for a guy.

I'D LIKE TO "AMEN" MYSELF. Guys will come and guys will go, but most friends are forever. To throw over a friend for some snacky *dude du jour* is, well, short-sighted. Think of it this way: you talk to your best friend about your boyfriend ad nauseum—right? But you don't talk to your boyfriend about your best friend the same way. So, if you 86'ed your best friend in favor of the boyfriend, who would you talk about the boyfriend with? Everyone knows you can have a best friend without a boyfriend, but you can't have a boyfriend without a best friend.

A GREAT FRIENDSHIP IS
ONE WHERE YOU DON'T
HAVE TO EXPLAIN
ANYTHING. NEED I SAY
MORE, FRIENDS?*

*Did ya get how clever I was there?

Have your moles checked. Skin cancer is so preventable, yet lots of people die from it or have to have big chunks of skin carved out because of it.

Being shy is no excuse.

PULL YOUR OWN WEIGHT WHEN TALKING TO PEOPLE, ESPECIALLY PEOPLE YOU DON'T KNOW. As I've mentioned before: *Everyone* loves to talk about themselves. Ask them questions about their life, their job—whatever! They'll come away thinking how cool you are, and you'll come away a little smarter.

The other thing people LOVE is a compliment. Say something like: "Do you know what I like about you?" Then make up something really fast like, *"I really like the fact that you . . . don't chew with your mouth open!"* (Now, there *is* a difference between really liking someone and being a suck-up, so only say it if you mean it.)

Smart girls are more interested in having fun than trying to look perfect.

I have this friend—let's just call her Jane. Jane's the kind of chick who's always the life of the party. She moves through a room like she *owns* it, and can talk to anyone. Anyway, I once said something to Jane about how easy it was for her to mingle, and how I wished it was as easy for me. Well, Jane got kind of miffed! She told me that it *wasn't* totally easy for her, and that she worked at being chatty and having fun things to say. Her not-so-subtle point was that I wasn't really being *shy*—I was being kind of lazy.

FAMILY

Everyone's
family is as
freaky
as yours.

Visit and/or talk to your grandparents as much as you can. Ask them to tell you stories about their lives. I guarantee you'll learn things that'll surprise you . . .

BUT EVERY FAMILY IS FREAKY IN ITS OWN UNIQUE WAY. Don't believe me? See the perfect family in this picture? Well, they're not so perfect. See the mom? The one who's all perfect and June Cleaver-like? Sent the family into bankruptcy with her cable-TV shopping addiction. Dear 'ole "straight-arrow" Dad? *Drag Queen.* Butch Brother? *Bed wetter.* God-fearing little girl? *Devil worshipper.* So you see, every family's got its secrets, even if they appear "normal" on the outside.

Keep a gratitude page. It's good to always stay in a place of gratitude, so we can really see how fortunate we are. Try to write at least one thing you're grateful for everyday.

Yes, they're clueless, but it won't kill you to play along.

Remember:

You *can* create a family apart from your natural one—sometimes a relief when the real one is driving you crazy or just doesn't understand you.

EVERYTHING IS POLITICAL. This is a "choose your battles" situation. If you take a sweater to school when Mom tells you to, even if it's, like, 120 degrees outside, you could win brownie points and get to go to the mall with Brittany after soccer practice.

Here's the way to do it: On your way out, hide the sweater in the bushes, and simply pick it up on your way back in. (Just hope the sprinklers don't go off while you're away.) Then everyone's happy—it's a win-win sitch. And later, when you catch a cold 'cause you didn't wear the sweater, you can tell Mom: *"See, I wore your stupid sweater and I'm still sick."* Then she might feel bad and buy you something you really want.

Like a pony.

Your mom will
always make
you crazy.

Take care of your knees.
Cause when they go, they're gone. Plus, it's awfully hard to rollerblade without them.

NOT TOO LONG AGO, I WITNESSED A RIP-ROARING FIGHT BETWEEN A NINETY-YEAR-OLD MOTHER AND A SEVENTY-YEAR-OLD DAUGHTER IN A WAL-MART PARKING LOT IN TOPEKA, KANSAS (MY HOME TOWN). The seventy year-old daughter had an honest-to-God tantrum in front of her little old lady mom.

I couldn't hear the mom, 'cause she was doing that passive-aggressive soft-talking thing. Like, *I'm rational and normal and you're crazy for screaming.* (Not that I have personal experience in this area, you understand. I was just an observer.) But anyway, it got so bad I thought the daughter was gonna hold her breath, turn blue and pass out right there on the blacktop. It was hilarious because they were older, but the point is that this mother/daughter thing can be intense no matter what your age.

Often times a fight about your tattoo isn't about that at all. Maybe it's really about your mom not liking your new best friend or maybe she's upset about you growing up and just can't confront the real issue. Your power and grace will come through as you try to be *conscious* about what's really going on between you and your mom. If you feel like your mom is pushing your buttons, take a breath first before you go off. Tell her you have to think about what she's saying and that you'll get back to her with an answer—anything to head off a fight. Then maybe the two of you can talk rationally later.

Don't whine.
Whining's for those who can't ask for what they want.

Brothers and
sisters are
extra special
friends.

MY MOM SAYS THAT WHEN SHE BROUGHT ANDREW, MY BROTHER, HOME FROM THE HOSPITAL, THE FIRST THING THAT CAME OUT OF MY TWO-YEAR-OLD MOUTH WAS: *"THROW HIM OUT THE WINDOW."* I guess you could say we got off on the wrong foot. Anyway, when we were kids we fought like crazy. My mom would play this record for us called, ***"Brothers and Sisters Are Extra Special Friends."***

Extra specially hateful, I thought, if I could think such a thing at five. The song was supposed to make us grateful to have each other, and we hated it. I remember Andrew throwing the little *Close 'n Play* record player across the room in disgust. Now, *that* brought us closer together than the stupid song, but I digress.

The deal is, our brothers and sisters will be with us (hopefully) long after our parents are gone. They share memories of our childhoods. They know you better than anyone, and can provide a real sense of intimacy. Studies have shown that people who have close relationships with their siblings live longer, happier, healthier lives. So, if you're close to your siblings now—cool, keep the relationship going. If not, try to reach out slowly—a card or letter—and see if it's reciprocated. Then progress from there. My brother and I are "extra special friends" now, and honestly, I don't know what I would do if he wasn't in my life.

Don't pluck! Wax or electrolysize for God's sake. It is the quick fix, but plucking only makes hair more coarse.

f you want a healthy glow, buy one from a bottle.

C'mon,
who else is
gonna make
your bail?

LOVE 'EM OR NOT, THE TRUTH IS YOUR FAMILY MEMBERS WILL PROBABLY BE THE ONES WHO'LL HELP YOU WHEN ALL ELSE FAILS. They'll be the ones to hold your broken hand at the hospital after your ill-fated attempt at winning the bucking bronco championship. They'll also be the ones who'll take out a third mortgage on the house to bail you out of a Mexican prison. Just knowing this could provide you with a feeling of security throughout your life—even if you never have to depend on it.

Never mistake knowledge for wisdom. One helps you make a living, the other helps you make a life.

—SANDRA CAREY

MONEY

Keep your
own purse.

THE DAY YOU DEPEND ON SOMEONE ELSE FOR FINANCIAL SUPPORT IS THE DAY YOU SAY ***BUH-BYE*** TO INDEPENDENCE. Always maintain the ability to take care of yourself, even if you're supported by your parents, your trust fund, or your life partner. The point is to never completely depend on another person for financial support. It's not a matter of trust, it's a matter of self-worth. There's confidence in knowing you can do for yourself should the need arise.

Amen.

I decided long ago never to look at the right hand of the menu or the price tag of clothes—otherwise I would starve, naked.

—HELEN HAYES

Smart girls know about $$

If you don't know anything about investing, ask a friend who does, take a class, see a investment counselor, or pick up a book.

There is a difference between being stupid and taking a calculated risk.

I'd like to have a chat with you about credit cards. Hey, please don't flip the page. I know this subject's a potential bore, but if you screw up your credit, it can be a real pain.

At one point in my life, I found myself in $20,000 worth of debt, and I really have no earthly idea how it happened. Sure, some of that debt was from student loans, but the other half . . . well, I just don't want any of you to make the same mistake I made. I was definitely stupid when it came to credit, and by *stupid* I mean racking up charges willy-nilly. You know—without a plan.

I saw a designer bag I loved and just had to have it. I wasn't making a lot of money at the time, so I charged it, rationalizing that *everyone else had a Prada bag, why couldn't I?** Plus a couple of trips to Vegas to catch Tom Jones (*Hey, it's not unusual*) and before I knew it, I owed twenty grand. Okay, so I also charged dinners, clothes, and expensive presents for lovers who no longer talk to me, but that's another story (and book). The point is that none of my debt was *calculated*.

*read with whiney voice

MORE ON

Popularity = conformity.

You can't be popular unless you fit in, and you can only fit in by being the same. Just know that the price you pay is high in suppressing who you really are.

The *calculated* part refers to those who have a plan:

> Say you've dreamed of being a movie maker your whole life. You have a great idea for a short film but for some odd reason, no one will front you the $20,000 you figure it will cost. After careful consideration, you put the movie on plastic (of course getting the lowest interest rates possible). Now you're taking a calculated risk.

Here's what might happen . . .

(a) Your film gets great buzz at The Sundance Film Festival, and ends up being your ticket to a exciting yet gut-wrenching career as a chick director in Hollywood, in which case you could easily pay back the twenty grand. ***Or***

(b) Your film doesn't win at Sundance, but you meet some producer types who think you have potential and offer you a job assisting a director on a feature (in which case you couldn't pay back the twenty grand in one shot, but you could definitely make your minimum payments). ***Or***

(c) Your film sucks and Robert Redford personally asks you to leave the festival and return your complimentary Sundance catalog. In which case you'll still be out the $20,000, but good or bad, at least you took the risk with your eyes wide open.

MONEY

Know your comfort levels with $$$.

I F YOU'RE THE TYPE OF GAL WHO CAN CHARGE TWENTY GRAND ON PLASTIC TO MAKE A MOVIE, AND NOT THINK TWICE ABOUT IT—COOL. But, if you're the type who could find yourself wakening with a start at two in the morning, heart pounding, in a cold sweat, balled up in the fetal position from a nightmare in which you're a bag lady who has nothing to eat but the cardboard box you've been living in . . . Well, I'm not a therapist, but perhaps dropping the twenty grand isn't for you.

"No one can arrive from being talented alone. God gives talent, work transforms talent into genius."

—Anna Pavlova

 Write down what you'd like to accomplish throughout the year. Then break down your goals by the month, then by the week. After all, you can't get what you want if you don't *know* what you want.

Friends don't let
friends borrow
money.

MONEY CAN BRING OUT THE BEST AND THE WORST IN PEOPLE. Unfortunately, when money's loaned or borrowed, it usually brings out the worst. It's the weirdest thing, but psychologically it pushes our emotional buttons. I've seen many a relationship hit the skids over unpaid loans. This is why, after experiencing both roles of borrower and lender, I recommend being neither. It may sound cold but if you never want to resent your lover/friend/cousin/brother/uncle, etc. you'll borrow from an impartial institution like a bank or credit card company. And you'll tell anyone who asks to borrow cash that you have a policy of never lending money.

SIDEBAR

If you feel generous and wish to give someone money as a *gift,* cool. But you should do so without any strings attached. Before giving anyone money, make sure you're pure of heart, and that you don't care how they spend it—*really*. If they've talked about paying off their bills, but spend the money on a trip to Tanzania to climb Mt. Kilimanjaro, it's their business.

SON OF SIDEBAR

Not to backpedal, but there *are* relationships which have no problems with the money issue. How about this as a rule of thumb? Make sure you've been friends for at least fifty years in this lifetime and have spent at least two previous lifetimes together. The bottom line is that you've got to be comfortable with the situation.

You can't follow
your dreams
if you can't
pay for the gas.

YOU KNOW, THERE ARE ONE OR TWO DRAWBACKS TO BEING AN ADULT. Along with independence and drinking legally comes the sad realization that you'll find stray hairs growing in really weird places and that you have to pay your own bills. The hair thing is easily taken care of by a little wax, but the bill thing? Well, what can I say—it's a big, old, fat buzzkill.

When I moved to New York to be an actress after high school, I thought I'd actually make a living being an actress. I was convinced the New York stage was awaiting my arrival. I didn't think for a moment that I'd have to work at a real job to make ends meet.

What a sad sad day it was to hear myself utter the words, *"Hi, I'm Mindy, and I'll be your server this evening."* But I had a dream, and so I sacrificed myself for stardom. I was ill-prepared to make a living in the real world. I had no viable skills besides chewing the scenery (and some would argue that point). I didn't know anything about computers or how to type or any of the so-called *survival jobs*. It took me a while to face reality and enroll myself in typing and computer classes, and a while longer to make enough money to have a relatively comfortable life.

It was only then that the feeling of desperation subsided and I got an agent and started auditioning. I did have some success as an actress in movies and TV, and now that I make a living as a writer, I can look back at the time I spent being an actress and think, *thank God I'm making a living as a writer.* And I had to be a writer's assistant for years to get where I am now. But I don't regret, can't forget, what I did for *my art*. After all, it got me to where I am now. And do you know what I'm totally proud of (besides the fact that I can get through a spinning class without throwing up)? It's that I was the kind of gal who could sling a few burgers to pay her rent. *That's* the mark of a real woman, my friends.

Don't be a
crybaby
negotiator.

Even beautiful babes on the cover of the fashion mags don't look like that in real life. A good air brush could make anyone's butt look perfect. Don't allow yourself to feel bad by falling for bogus marketing campaigns. Remember, advertisers want you to feel bad so you'll buy their products.

YOU DON'T GET IF YOU DON'T ASK. I have this friend. (Yes, that's right. A friend. As in not me.) Anyway, I have this friend who is an executive. Several other executives at her level got promotions and raises, but my friend didn't. She was pissed, and rightly so. She had won the equivalent of the Oscar in her field for God's sake, and brought in millions of dollars in revenue. *What does a girl have to do to get recognition around here?*, she thought.

Apparently, she had to ask for her own damn raise her own damn self. Unbeknownst to her, that's what the other execs had done. She was so hurt and angry by the time she asked her boss for her well deserved raise, she burst into tears. This made the boss uncomfortable and totally embarrassed my friend. It's hard to negotiate effectively with mascara and/or snot running down your face.

Now I'm not one to dis someone for crying, but there's a time and place for everything. Just try to get your crying and anger out before you go in. And invest in some smudge proof mascara while you're at it.

Benjamin Franklin once said, "Never a borrower nor a lender be."

Did you know old Ben was considered the father of our country? I heard that he was *literally* the father of our country 'cause he fathered so many kids. He apparently had a way of *conducting electricity* with the lassies. Get it?—electricity 'cause Ben also did the key on the kite thing, remember? I thought it was Hi-larious. Oh well.

While you're
at it,
ask for
double the raise.

If someone continuously pisses you off, it's time to look at yourself. Why else would they piss you off so much?

OKAY, YOU KNOW MY FRIEND FROM BEFORE? She taught us Rule #1 about negotiating, which is . . . Anyone . . . ? Anyone . . . ? *No crying.* Be calm. Meditate if you have to. Take a yoga class, whatever it takes before you go in.

But now let's review another important negotiating rule from your Aunt Mindy. Keep this one to yourself! Rule #2 is: **Start by asking for twice as much as you really want.**

That's right, girlfriend. You're not being a witch—you're just playing the age-old game of negotiating. Next, your boss will probably low-ball you, offering you much less than you deserve. Hey, don't get pissed! Remember Rule #1, ladies! (No need to check back, you lazy bums. It's *stay calm,* remember? Jeez).

Now, you come back with a slightly lower number than your original offer . . . and so on and so on until one of you has an aneurysm. Be really cool and polite, but professional. Stand tough. More times than not, you'll get more than you thought you would.

P.S. The same advice goes for buying a car, but an amendment to the above is that, in this scenario, you're the boss.

Don't declare bankruptcy

If you find yourself over your head with credit cards, contact Consumer Credit Counseling Services. They'll call your creditors and help you reduce your interest rates and payments. If you declare bankruptcy, it remains on your credit for seven years. Bye-bye to buying a house, bye-bye to buying a car or anything you can't pay for in cash. Take responsibility for your own spending.

LIFE

TIPS

Learn to be alone!

IT'S IMPORTANT TO BE ABLE TO ENJOY TIME ALONE. People sense it when you need them too much, and they tend to back away. (Unfortunately, desperation is not pretty or I'd be Miss America.) So you need to cultivate a relationship with *you*. Nothing is more attractive than a woman who is content being on her own. The goal is to progress to a place where you can always count on yourself to have fun. Find activities or hobbies to do alone.

Well, there are the old standbys: reading, writing, drawing, and painting. But let's explore some less obvious activities:

- **Start your own zine.** A zine is a hand-made publication that combines elements of personal journals, newsletters and magazines. It's a great way to discover the writer in you. Please refer to *Zine Scene* (The Do-It-Yourself Guide to Zines) written by Francesca Lia Block & Hillary Carlip.
- **Start your own band.** Okay, you need other people for this, but if you want something to do by yourself, learn an instrument. That's how lots of grrl rockers got started, like Ani DiFranco, MeShell Ndegéocello, and Alanis Morissette.
- **Start your own business.** You can run your own company *now,* making money by washing cars or designing your own jewelry. Please refer to *Girl Boss* written by Stacy Kravetz.
- **Write your own play/Make your own video.** It could be something totally fictional (something you make up) or biographical (about your life or someone else's). If you write your own play, you could also produce and direct it. Cast your friends, have rehearsals, invite an audience, make programs. The same goes for the video. It could be a music video, a TV show or a short movie. Write a script, plan your shots, draw storyboards, cast your friends, shoot, and edit.

Cool chicks travel! It broadens your horizons. Dream about the trips you'd like to take. Look up different countries on the web or in catalogs. Start saving your money. You don't have to travel expensively to have fun.

This is the best part of the head cheerleader's life.

DON'T SWEAT IT IF HER HAIR LOOKS BETTER, OR HER BOYFRIEND IS FINER. Chances are, she's peaked while you still have buttloads of time to do great things.

> *Women whose identity depends more on their outsides than their insides are dangerous when they begin to age.*
>
> —Gloria Steinem

Grades really do matter.

HERE'S THE DEAL—YOU'LL NEVER USE TRIGONOMETRY AGAIN. Ever. I never used it when I had it. But the grade you make in class will count when applying to colleges. It's stupid, I know, but that's the way the world works. And who knows—you might be on *Jeopardy* one day, and knowing the Pythagorean theorem could be the difference between being champion or just another bloated, badly dressed egghead from Fresno. (Note to self: Look up Pythagorean theorem).

Stretch before you work out. Be nice to your muscles and they'll be nice to you . . .

Be happy. It is a way of being wise.

—COLETTE

Everyone
gets
bummed
out.

Exercise. It's good for your mind, body, spirit and self-esteem. Make sure to have fun—think about what makes you *feel* good—not what makes you look good.

IT'S NORMAL TO FEEL BAD FROM TIME TO TIME. Sometimes we don't get what we want, it disappoints us and it gets us down. Sometimes things happen to us that are out of our control that bum us out—i.e., the guy you like only digs girls over seven feet tall or something. It happens.

And when it does, we tend to pull away from our friends and family and stop talking. And sometimes we *don't know* what's going on—we only know that life sucks. But it's important that you do talk to someone—a friend, teacher, whomever—about what's going on. Now, if you find you're *really down* all the time, you might be depressed. In that case, it may be time to seek professional help. Ask your school counselor or your parents about talking to a therapist—it's no biggie, it happens to the best of us.

Happiness is good health and a bad memory.

—INGRID BERGMAN

It's worth spending $50, 000 on psychotherapy to feel better about your nose than to pay $10, 000 for a nose job.

Take a 2nd look
at the
dweeb.

Volunteer. You'll learn skills that the for-profit world isn't willing to teach you. Plus, you're doing a good deed.

YOU KNOW THE DWEEB YOU MAKE FUN OF FOR EATING CRAYONS, PAPER WRAPPERS AND ALL? Well, he's probably the one most likely to be a brilliant billionaire later in life . . . At least that's what Bill Gates's classmates said.

If high heels were so wonderful, men would be wearing them.

—SUE GRAFTON

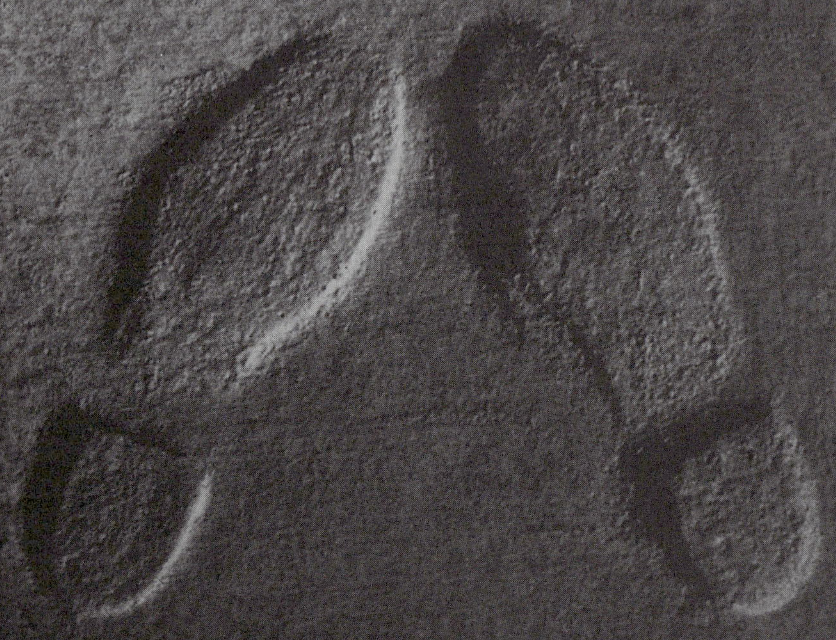

Stamp out your inner critic.

FIGURE OUT THE WAYS THAT YOU SABOTAGE YOURSELF WITH SELF-FULFILLING PROPHESIES—I.E., *I CAN'T GET INTO HARVARD BECAUSE I'M TOO SHORT, TOO STUPID, FEMALE, GAY, BLACK, WHATEVER.*

We can be our own worst enemies. Think about how you trip yourself up, and consciously decide to put an end to it. *Retrain your mind.* You once told yourself a story about how you weren't good enough, and now you're going to tell yourself a story about how it's your birthright to be a happy, successful worthy person. So, tell that inner critic to take a hike.

Don't put your underwear in the dryer . . . It cuts the life of your delicates in half.

The person who tells you to celebrate your period has never had one.
Period.

Having a manicure/pedicure is an inexpensive way to feel good about yourself and have healthy cuticles. And nothing's more sexy than a girl with healthy cuticles.

YOU KNOW THOSE "FEMININE PRODUCT" COMMERCIALS ON TELEVISION—THE ONES THAT SHOW LOTS OF CHICKS JOYFULLY RUNNING AROUND IN WHITE, SO HAPPY TO BE MENSTRUATING GALS-ON-THE-GO? It's crap. All of it. Men must be writing those commercials, because having a period—well, it sucks, plain and simple. (And shouldn't it be called *womenstrating* anyway?) But don't lose hope, 'cause the good news is, after a while you get into a routine and you figure it out for yourself. Soon you realize that there's no reason that you and your period can't be friends.

When I started my period at twelve and a half, I remember it being a horrifying experience. I felt my body was betraying me somehow. ("*What do you mean I can't go swimming?*") But after some time I figured out how to interpret the warning signs of its arrival, and kinda go, "*Oh, I'm getting my period. Whatever.*" And you'll likely do the same thing.

You'll begin to understand how to plan for it by filling up your purse with everything you need ahead of time: feminine supplies, aspirin, perhaps a gun. And then after some time, you'll graduate from "riding the cotton pony" to using tampons, which totally changes your life. ("*You mean, I* can *go swimming?*")

Learn another language.

Just When You

Period Tip #1

You should also know that periods can really be a painful experience for some girls. I know a girl who can't get out of bed when she's having hers. I also know I've been in *total* pain from time to time and found relief in acupuncture and Chinese herbs. So if you're in pain, you don't have to live that way—there's help out there! Figure out your individual tonic—whether its acupuncture, ibuprofen, chocolate, or all three. Sometimes a girl just wants to lie in bed with her heating pad and complain.

Thought I'd

Get a pelvic exam at least once a year. Yeah, it can be a bitch, but since you've been blessed with a vag, you gotta take responsibility for it. If you feel uncomfortable, find a chick gyno, and tell her how you feel. Gynos not only prescribe birth control, they check for cervical cancer and

Period Tip #2

The other thing is that periods can *really* alter your moods. You can totally be affected by all of those hormones raging around in your body. I know you've heard those stupid PMS jokes, but there's something to it. I, for example, always forget when I'm pre-menstrual. Sometimes I fly off the handle about something that normally wouldn't phase me at all, or I'll cry at the drop of a hat and won't know why. So when I'm pre-menstrual I try to remind myself that I'm a healthy woman going through a perfectly natural experience and that it's cool to have these hormonal changes. And dammit, we as women should celebrate this, instead of feeling negative about it! Then maybe it wouldn't be such a pain.

AH . . . PERIOD MEMORIES

When I was in high school, my friends and I kept our tampons in our sunglass cases, and if we needed to borrow one (which always happened in choir for some reason—I think we were all in the alto section), we had a special code, which was, *"Boy, it's sunny today. Could I borrow your sunglasses, Marla?"*

Be who you are!

FRIENDS ARE THOSE WHO ARE SUPPORTIVE AND HELPFUL. If you find you have people surrounding you who vampire your kindness or who try to make you feel bad about yourself, I have two words of advice, *Buh-bye.*

You can't change the music of your soul.

—KATHARINE HEPBURN

Fold your clothes while they're still warm from the dryer. That way they won't get so wrinkly and they'll retain a perfect crease.

Debate's
da bomb.

YOU KNOW, THERE ARE MANY BENEFITS TO TAKING DEBATE BESIDES GETTING TO KNOW ALL THE PIMPLE-FACED GEEKS IN YOUR CLASS. If you have aspirations to be a lawyer or plan to be married, debate teaches you to represent an argument from both sides of an issue. I know, it's a dweebapalooza. But it will also help you take control of a meeting in one of those cool looking boardrooms, or give a speech at the Oscars or the United Nations.

Chicks who can express themselves intelligently are cool, powerful—and usually end up rich.

And do we have to say anything about drugs? Haven't you heard enough already? Don't be a loser.

Attitude is all. A couple of friends have asked me if I've lost weight and to tell you the truth, I haven't, but I tell them I have. Recently I've begun to feel great about myself and it shows. Now THAT's a powerful 'tude, my friends.

Stop obsessing
about your weight.

YOU KNOW WHAT I'D REALLY LIKE? To have all the time I've worried about my weight given back to me. I'm sure it would total five or six years of needless, ridiculous imprisoning thoughts about how I was too fat to be desired by anyone. Oh, it makes me sad just writing about it.

Just recently, I looked through some photographs that were taken three or four years ago, and I thought how cute, snacky and slim I looked. But I remember seeing those photos when they were taken, and thinking that I looked hideous and fat. See what I mean? Perspective is everything, my friends. It's not that I have this negative thinking thing conquered, but I'm more *aware* of it now. So when I catch myself thinking that I'm not thin enough, I remind myself to dismiss it and replace it with a positive thought.

Listen—I try to be conscious about what and how much I eat, but I LIKE to eat, dammit! I'm not giving it up. I exercise to keep in shape but that's as far as I'm going. And that's what all of us should do! Once you learn to accept your own looks, you'll be amazed at how others will learn to accept you too.

You're likely to always be about this same weight. (Unless you're the writer of this book. In which case you'll have a wardrobe for a smaller-sized "me" and larger-sized "somebody else.")

Life itself is the proper binge.

—JULIA CHILD

Win free money now.

SORRY, THAT'S NOT WHAT THIS PARAGRAPH IS ABOUT, BUT I THOUGHT YOU WOULDN'T LOOK AT A PARAGRAPH ENTITLED "KEEP GOOD RECORDS." So, now that I have your attention, it really *is* important to keep good records. That's because if there's a mistake on someone else's part (or some company's part), you'll have your own proof.

Keep a diary. It helps when you need to vent, or when you're trying to figure something out. Also, it's a kick to keep your old journals and read them years later. It'll kill you to read about what you were going through when you were eight, ten, twelve, etc. and give you insight about who you are now.

Once you start filing your own taxes, the IRS can audit your for up to seven years, so keep everything until then.

Available from Girl Press

Cool Women: Original Divas
All-True Tales from the World's Most Fabulous Stage & Screen Divas
$9.00
1-931497-04-4

"When I'm good I'm very good, when I'm bad, I'm better."
—Mae West

Before there was Madonna there was Mae West. Discover the inside stories of the women who pushed the envelope, dared to be daring, and changed the way we looked at women entertainers. From Josephine Baker to Carmen Miranda to Lillie Langtry, these Cool Women knew how to command an audience.

Girl Director
A How-To Guide for the First-Time, Flat-Broke Film Maker (and Video Maker)
by Andrea Richards
$17.95
1-931497-00-1

"Directing. It's such a good job for girls."
—Betty Thomas

Women film directors are everywhere, and *Girl Director* is here to help the next generation of filmmakers learn the ropes. A fun, hip and irreverent how-to guide, *Girl Director* is chock full of facts, tips and lessons from working women directors. With an introduction by director Alison Anders (*Gas Food Lodging, Four Rooms*).